50 American BBQ Styles to Master

By: Kelly Johnson

Table of Contents

- Texas Brisket
- Kansas City Ribs
- Memphis Pulled Pork
- North Carolina Whole Hog
- South Carolina Mustard BBQ
- St. Louis Style Ribs
- Alabama White Sauce BBQ
- Carolina Style BBQ Chicken
- Texas Sausage
- Tennessee Smoked Turkey
- Kansas City Burnt Ends
- Memphis Style Dry Ribs
- Oklahoma Joe's BBQ
- Western North Carolina Vinegar BBQ
- Chicago Style BBQ
- South Carolina Shrimp and Grits BBQ
- BBQ Brisket Tacos
- Texas-Style BBQ Beans
- Smoky BBQ Meatloaf
- Buffalo Style BBQ Chicken Wings
- California BBQ Tri-Tip
- Hawaiian BBQ Pork
- New York Style BBQ
- Texas-Style BBQ Chicken
- Deep South BBQ Shrimp
- Low Country Boil BBQ
- BBQ Beef Short Ribs
- Alabama Style Chicken
- BBQ Pulled Jackfruit
- BBQ Venison
- Maple-Glazed BBQ Salmon
- BBQ Pork Chops
- BBQ Lamb Ribs
- BBQ Flatbread Pizzas
- Cajun BBQ Shrimp

- BBQ Spatchcock Chicken
- BBQ Pork Belly
- BBQ Beer Can Chicken
- BBQ Baked Potatoes
- BBQ Nachos
- BBQ Bacon-Wrapped Jalapeños
- BBQ Stuffed Peppers
- BBQ Sweet Potato Wedges
- BBQ Burger Sliders
- BBQ Fajitas
- BBQ Meatball Subs
- BBQ Mac and Cheese
- BBQ Pulled Pork Sandwiches
- BBQ Deviled Eggs
- BBQ Dessert Pizza

Texas Sausage

Ingredients:

- 2 lbs ground beef
- 1 lb pork fat
- 1 tablespoon kosher salt
- 1 tablespoon black pepper
- 1 tablespoon garlic powder
- 1 tablespoon paprika
- 1 teaspoon cayenne pepper
- Sausage casings

Instructions:

1. **Prepare the Sausage Mixture**
   In a large bowl, combine ground beef, pork fat, and spices. Mix well until the meat is sticky.
2. **Stuff the Casings**
   Rinse sausage casings and stuff with the meat mixture, tying off at regular intervals.
3. **Cook the Sausage**
   Smoke the sausages at 225°F for about 3-4 hours until they reach an internal temperature of 160°F.

Tennessee Smoked Turkey

Ingredients:

- 1 whole turkey (12-14 lbs)
- 1/4 cup olive oil
- 1/4 cup dry rub (paprika, garlic powder, onion powder, brown sugar)
- 1 cup apple juice

Instructions:

1. **Prepare the Turkey**
   Rinse the turkey and pat dry. Rub with olive oil and then apply the dry rub evenly over the skin.
2. **Smoke the Turkey**
   Preheat smoker to 225°F. Place turkey in the smoker, injecting with apple juice periodically. Smoke for about 6-8 hours, or until the internal temperature reaches 165°F.

Kansas City Burnt Ends

Ingredients:

- 4 lbs brisket point
- 1/4 cup rub (brown sugar, paprika, garlic powder, salt)
- 1 cup BBQ sauce

Instructions:

1. **Season the Brisket**
   Rub the brisket point with the spice mix and let it sit for at least 1 hour.
2. **Smoke the Brisket**
   Smoke at 225°F for 6-8 hours until tender. Remove and let rest.
3. **Cube and Sauce**
   Cut into cubes, toss with BBQ sauce, and return to the smoker for an additional 1-2 hours.

Memphis Style Dry Ribs

Ingredients:

- 2 racks of baby back ribs
- 1/4 cup dry rub (paprika, cayenne pepper, black pepper, salt)
- 1/4 cup apple juice

Instructions:

1. **Prepare the Ribs**
   Remove the membrane from the back of the ribs and apply the dry rub evenly.
2. **Smoke the Ribs**
   Smoke at 225°F for 4-5 hours, spritzing with apple juice every hour.
3. **Finish**
   Remove from smoker and let rest for 10 minutes before serving without sauce.

Oklahoma Joe's BBQ

Ingredients:

- 2 lbs pork shoulder
- 1/4 cup BBQ rub (paprika, brown sugar, chili powder)
- 1/2 cup apple cider vinegar
- 1/2 cup BBQ sauce

Instructions:

1. **Season the Pork**
   Rub the pork shoulder with BBQ rub and let sit for at least 1 hour.
2. **Smoke the Pork**
   Smoke at 225°F for 8-10 hours until the internal temperature reaches 195°F.
3. **Pull and Serve**
   Shred the pork and mix with apple cider vinegar and BBQ sauce before serving.

Western North Carolina Vinegar BBQ

Ingredients:

- 2 lbs pork shoulder
- 1 cup apple cider vinegar
- 1/4 cup red pepper flakes
- 1 tablespoon salt
- 1 tablespoon black pepper

Instructions:

1. **Prepare the Pork**
   Rub the pork shoulder with salt and pepper.
2. **Smoke the Pork**
   Smoke at 225°F for about 8 hours, basting with a mixture of vinegar and red pepper flakes.
3. **Serve**
   Shred the pork and serve with additional vinegar sauce.

Chicago Style BBQ

Ingredients:

- 3 lbs beef ribs
- 1/4 cup dry rub (brown sugar, garlic powder, onion powder)
- 1 cup BBQ sauce

Instructions:

1. **Season the Ribs**
   Apply the dry rub evenly over the beef ribs.
2. **Cook the Ribs**
   Cook in a smoker or grill at 250°F for 5-6 hours, applying BBQ sauce during the last hour.
3. **Serve**
   Let rest before slicing and serving.

South Carolina Shrimp and Grits BBQ

Ingredients:

- 1 lb shrimp, peeled and deveined
- 1 cup grits
- 2 cups chicken broth
- 1/2 cup BBQ sauce
- 1/4 cup chopped green onions

Instructions:

1. **Prepare the Grits**
   Cook grits in chicken broth according to package instructions.
2. **Cook the Shrimp**
   In a pan, sauté shrimp until pink, then mix with BBQ sauce.
3. **Serve**
   Serve shrimp over grits, garnished with green onions.

BBQ Brisket Tacos

Ingredients:

- 2 lbs brisket
- 1 tablespoon BBQ rub (smoked paprika, garlic powder, onion powder)
- 1 cup beef broth
- Corn tortillas
- Fresh cilantro and lime for garnish

Instructions:

1. **Prepare the Brisket**
   Rub brisket with BBQ rub and let it rest for at least 1 hour.
2. **Cook the Brisket**
   Place brisket in a slow cooker with beef broth. Cook on low for 8-10 hours until tender.
3. **Shred and Serve**
   Shred the brisket and serve in corn tortillas, topped with cilantro and a squeeze of lime.

Texas-Style BBQ Beans

Ingredients:

- 1 can (15 oz) pinto beans, drained and rinsed
- 1 can (15 oz) black beans, drained and rinsed
- 1/2 cup BBQ sauce
- 1/2 cup chopped onion
- 1 tablespoon Worcestershire sauce

Instructions:

1. **Combine Ingredients**
   In a pot, combine all ingredients and mix well.
2. **Simmer**
   Simmer on low heat for 20-30 minutes until heated through.
3. **Serve**
   Serve warm as a side dish.

Smoky BBQ Meatloaf

Ingredients:

- 2 lbs ground beef
- 1 cup breadcrumbs
- 1/2 cup BBQ sauce
- 1/2 cup chopped onion
- 1 egg
- 1 tablespoon smoked paprika

Instructions:

1. **Preheat Oven**
   Preheat the oven to 350°F (175°C).
2. **Mix Ingredients**
   In a bowl, combine all ingredients until well mixed.
3. **Shape and Bake**
   Shape into a loaf and place in a baking dish. Bake for 1 hour, brushing with additional BBQ sauce halfway through.

Buffalo Style BBQ Chicken Wings

Ingredients:

- 2 lbs chicken wings
- 1/2 cup buffalo sauce
- 1 tablespoon melted butter
- Celery sticks and blue cheese dressing for serving

Instructions:

1. **Preheat Oven**
   Preheat the oven to 400°F (200°C).
2. **Prepare the Wings**
   Toss chicken wings with buffalo sauce and melted butter.
3. **Bake**
   Spread wings on a baking sheet and bake for 40-45 minutes until crispy. Serve with celery and blue cheese.

California BBQ Tri-Tip

Ingredients:

- 2 lbs tri-tip roast
- 1/4 cup olive oil
- 2 tablespoons garlic powder
- 1 tablespoon black pepper
- 1 tablespoon kosher salt

Instructions:

1. **Season the Tri-Tip**
   Rub the tri-tip with olive oil, garlic powder, black pepper, and salt.
2. **Grill the Tri-Tip**
   Preheat grill to medium-high heat. Grill tri-tip for 30-40 minutes, flipping halfway, until desired doneness.
3. **Rest and Slice**
   Let rest for 10 minutes before slicing against the grain.

Hawaiian BBQ Pork

Ingredients:

- 2 lbs pork shoulder
- 1/4 cup soy sauce
- 1/4 cup brown sugar
- 1/4 cup pineapple juice
- 1 tablespoon garlic minced

Instructions:

1. **Prepare the Marinade**
   In a bowl, combine soy sauce, brown sugar, pineapple juice, and garlic.
2. **Marinate the Pork**
   Marinate pork shoulder in the mixture for at least 2 hours, or overnight.
3. **Cook**
   Roast in a slow cooker on low for 8-10 hours until tender. Shred and serve.

New York Style BBQ

Ingredients:

- 2 lbs beef ribs
- 1/4 cup dry rub (salt, pepper, paprika)
- 1 cup BBQ sauce

Instructions:

1. **Season the Ribs**
   Rub the beef ribs with the dry rub.
2. **Cook the Ribs**
   Cook ribs on a grill or smoker at 250°F (120°C) for 5-6 hours.
3. **Sauce and Serve**
   Brush with BBQ sauce during the last hour and serve.

Texas-Style BBQ Chicken

Ingredients:

- 2 lbs chicken pieces
- 1/4 cup BBQ rub (paprika, chili powder, garlic powder)
- 1 cup BBQ sauce

Instructions:

1. **Season the Chicken**
   Rub chicken pieces with BBQ rub and let sit for at least 30 minutes.
2. **Grill the Chicken**
   Grill chicken over medium heat for 30-40 minutes, turning occasionally.
3. **Finish with Sauce**
   Brush with BBQ sauce during the last 10 minutes of grilling.

Deep South BBQ Shrimp

Ingredients:

- 1 lb large shrimp, peeled and deveined
- 1/4 cup olive oil
- 1 tablespoon Worcestershire sauce
- 1 tablespoon lemon juice
- 2 cloves garlic, minced
- 1 tablespoon Cajun seasoning

Instructions:

1. **Marinate the Shrimp**
   In a bowl, combine olive oil, Worcestershire sauce, lemon juice, garlic, and Cajun seasoning. Add shrimp and marinate for 30 minutes.
2. **Cook the Shrimp**
   Preheat a grill or skillet over medium-high heat. Cook shrimp for 2-3 minutes per side until pink and cooked through.
3. **Serve**
   Serve hot with additional lemon wedges and your favorite sides.

Low Country Boil BBQ

Ingredients:

- 2 lbs shrimp, deveined
- 1 lb small potatoes
- 1 lb corn, cut into halves
- 1/4 cup Old Bay seasoning
- 1/2 lb sausage, sliced

Instructions:

1. **Boil the Potatoes**
   In a large pot, bring water to a boil. Add potatoes and boil for 10 minutes.
2. **Add Corn and Sausage**
   Add corn and sausage; cook for an additional 5 minutes.
3. **Add Shrimp**
   Add shrimp and Old Bay seasoning; cook for 3-5 minutes until shrimp are pink. Drain and serve.

BBQ Beef Short Ribs

Ingredients:

- 3 lbs beef short ribs
- 1/4 cup dry rub (brown sugar, paprika, garlic powder)
- 1 cup BBQ sauce

Instructions:

1. **Season the Ribs**
   Rub the short ribs with the dry rub and let sit for at least 1 hour.
2. **Cook the Ribs**
   Preheat grill or smoker to 250°F (120°C). Cook ribs for 4-5 hours until tender.
3. **Finish with Sauce**
   Brush with BBQ sauce during the last hour of cooking. Let rest before serving.

Alabama Style Chicken

Ingredients:

- 4 chicken quarters
- 1/4 cup white BBQ sauce (mayonnaise, vinegar, lemon juice)
- Salt and pepper to taste

Instructions:

1. **Season the Chicken**
   Season chicken with salt and pepper.
2. **Grill the Chicken**
   Preheat grill to medium heat. Grill chicken for 30-40 minutes until cooked through, basting with white BBQ sauce.
3. **Serve**
   Serve hot with extra sauce on the side.

BBQ Pulled Jackfruit

Ingredients:

- 2 cans young green jackfruit in water
- 1/2 cup BBQ sauce
- 1 tablespoon olive oil
- 1 onion, chopped
- 2 cloves garlic, minced

Instructions:

1. **Prepare the Jackfruit**
   Drain and rinse jackfruit. Remove seeds and shred the fruit.
2. **Cook the Jackfruit**
   In a skillet, heat olive oil over medium heat. Sauté onion and garlic until soft. Add jackfruit and BBQ sauce; cook for 15-20 minutes, stirring frequently.
3. **Serve**
   Serve on buns with coleslaw.

BBQ Venison

Ingredients:

- 2 lbs venison steaks
- 1/4 cup BBQ rub (paprika, salt, pepper)
- 1 cup BBQ sauce

Instructions:

1. **Season the Venison**
   Rub venison steaks with BBQ rub and let rest for at least 30 minutes.
2. **Grill the Steaks**
   Preheat grill to medium-high heat. Grill venison for 6-8 minutes per side, basting with BBQ sauce.
3. **Serve**
   Let rest for a few minutes before slicing. Serve with additional BBQ sauce.

Maple-Glazed BBQ Salmon

Ingredients:

- 2 salmon fillets
- 1/4 cup maple syrup
- 2 tablespoons soy sauce
- 1 tablespoon Dijon mustard
- Salt and pepper to taste

Instructions:

1. **Prepare the Marinade**
   In a bowl, whisk together maple syrup, soy sauce, and Dijon mustard.
2. **Marinate the Salmon**
   Place salmon in a shallow dish and pour marinade over it. Let marinate for 30 minutes.
3. **Grill the Salmon**
   Preheat grill to medium heat. Grill salmon skin-side down for 5-7 minutes, basting with marinade. Serve immediately.

BBQ Pork Chops

Ingredients:

- 4 pork chops
- 1/4 cup BBQ rub (brown sugar, chili powder)
- 1 cup BBQ sauce

Instructions:

1. **Season the Chops**
   Rub pork chops with BBQ rub and let sit for 30 minutes.
2. **Grill the Chops**
   Preheat grill to medium-high heat. Grill chops for 5-7 minutes per side, brushing with BBQ sauce during the last few minutes.
3. **Serve**
   Let rest for a few minutes before serving.

BBQ Lamb Ribs

Ingredients:

- 2 lbs lamb ribs
- 1/4 cup olive oil
- 2 tablespoons rosemary, chopped
- 2 tablespoons garlic powder
- Salt and pepper to taste
- 1 cup BBQ sauce

Instructions:

1. **Prepare the Ribs**
   Preheat grill to medium heat. Rub lamb ribs with olive oil, rosemary, garlic powder, salt, and pepper.
2. **Grill the Ribs**
   Place ribs on the grill, bone-side down, and cook for 2-3 hours, basting with BBQ sauce every 30 minutes.
3. **Serve**
   Let rest before serving with additional BBQ sauce.

BBQ Flatbread Pizzas

Ingredients:

- 4 flatbreads
- 1 cup BBQ sauce
- 2 cups shredded cheese (mozzarella, cheddar)
- Toppings of choice (grilled chicken, onions, peppers)

Instructions:

1. **Preheat Grill**
   Preheat grill to medium-high heat.
2. **Assemble Pizzas**
   Spread BBQ sauce on each flatbread, sprinkle with cheese, and add desired toppings.
3. **Grill the Pizzas**
   Place flatbreads on the grill and cook for 5-7 minutes until cheese is melted and bubbly.
4. **Serve**
   Slice and serve hot.

Cajun BBQ Shrimp

Ingredients:

- 1 lb large shrimp, peeled and deveined
- 1/4 cup Cajun seasoning
- 1/4 cup olive oil
- 2 cloves garlic, minced
- 1 tablespoon Worcestershire sauce

Instructions:

1. **Marinate the Shrimp**
   In a bowl, combine shrimp, Cajun seasoning, olive oil, garlic, and Worcestershire sauce. Let marinate for 30 minutes.
2. **Cook the Shrimp**
   Preheat grill to medium-high heat. Skewer shrimp and grill for 2-3 minutes per side until pink.
3. **Serve**
   Serve hot with a squeeze of lemon.

BBQ Spatchcock Chicken

Ingredients:

- 1 whole chicken (3-4 lbs)
- 1/4 cup olive oil
- 2 tablespoons smoked paprika
- 1 tablespoon garlic powder
- Salt and pepper to taste
- 1 cup BBQ sauce

Instructions:

1. **Prepare the Chicken**
   Preheat grill to medium heat. Spatchcock the chicken by removing the backbone and flattening it.
2. **Season the Chicken**
   Rub the chicken with olive oil, paprika, garlic powder, salt, and pepper.
3. **Grill the Chicken**
   Place the chicken skin-side down on the grill. Cook for 45-60 minutes, flipping halfway and basting with BBQ sauce.
4. **Serve**
   Let rest before slicing and serving with additional BBQ sauce.

BBQ Pork Belly

Ingredients:

- 2 lbs pork belly, skin scored
- 1/4 cup BBQ rub (brown sugar, chili powder)
- 1 cup BBQ sauce

Instructions:

1. **Season the Pork Belly**
   Rub pork belly with BBQ rub and let it sit for at least 1 hour.
2. **Cook the Pork Belly**
   Preheat grill to low heat (about 225°F or 107°C). Place pork belly on the grill, skin-side up, and cook for 3-4 hours until tender.
3. **Finish with Sauce**
   Brush with BBQ sauce during the last 30 minutes of cooking. Let rest before slicing.
4. **Serve**
   Serve with additional BBQ sauce.

BBQ Beer Can Chicken

Ingredients:

- 1 whole chicken (3-4 lbs)
- 1 can beer (or soda)
- 1/4 cup BBQ rub (salt, paprika, garlic powder)
- 1 cup BBQ sauce

Instructions:

1. **Prepare the Chicken**
   Preheat grill to medium heat. Season chicken inside and out with BBQ rub.
2. **Insert the Beer Can**
   Open the beer can and place it inside the chicken's cavity.
3. **Grill the Chicken**
   Place the chicken upright on the grill and cook for 1-1.5 hours until the internal temperature reaches 165°F (74°C). Baste with BBQ sauce during the last 15 minutes.
4. **Serve**
   Carefully remove the beer can and let the chicken rest before serving.

BBQ Baked Potatoes

Ingredients:

- 4 large russet potatoes
- 1/4 cup olive oil
- Salt and pepper to taste
- 1 cup shredded cheese
- Sour cream and chives for serving

Instructions:

1. **Prepare the Potatoes**
   Preheat grill to medium heat. Rub potatoes with olive oil, salt, and pepper.
2. **Grill the Potatoes**
   Wrap potatoes in aluminum foil and place them on the grill. Cook for 45-60 minutes, turning occasionally, until tender.
3. **Finish and Serve**
   Unwrap and top with cheese, sour cream, and chives before serving.

BBQ Nachos

Ingredients:

- 1 bag tortilla chips
- 1 cup shredded cheese (cheddar, Monterey Jack)
- 1 cup pulled pork or chicken
- 1/2 cup BBQ sauce
- Toppings (jalapeños, sour cream, green onions)

Instructions:

1. **Assemble the Nachos**
   On a baking sheet, layer tortilla chips, cheese, pulled pork, and drizzle with BBQ sauce.
2. **Grill the Nachos**
   Preheat grill to medium heat. Place the baking sheet on the grill and cook for 5-7 minutes until cheese is melted.
3. **Add Toppings and Serve**
   Remove from the grill and top with jalapeños, sour cream, and green onions before serving.

BBQ Lamb Ribs

Ingredients:

- 2 lbs lamb ribs
- 1/4 cup olive oil
- 2 tablespoons rosemary, chopped
- 2 tablespoons garlic powder
- Salt and pepper to taste
- 1 cup BBQ sauce

Instructions:

1. **Prepare the Ribs**
   Preheat grill to medium heat. Rub lamb ribs with olive oil, rosemary, garlic powder, salt, and pepper.
2. **Grill the Ribs**
   Place ribs on the grill, bone-side down, and cook for 2-3 hours, basting with BBQ sauce every 30 minutes.
3. **Serve**
   Let rest before serving with additional BBQ sauce.

BBQ Flatbread Pizzas

Ingredients:

- 4 flatbreads
- 1 cup BBQ sauce
- 2 cups shredded cheese (mozzarella, cheddar)
- Toppings of choice (grilled chicken, onions, peppers)

Instructions:

1. **Preheat Grill**
   Preheat grill to medium-high heat.
2. **Assemble Pizzas**
   Spread BBQ sauce on each flatbread, sprinkle with cheese, and add desired toppings.
3. **Grill the Pizzas**
   Place flatbreads on the grill and cook for 5-7 minutes until cheese is melted and bubbly.
4. **Serve**
   Slice and serve hot.

Cajun BBQ Shrimp

Ingredients:

- 1 lb large shrimp, peeled and deveined
- 1/4 cup Cajun seasoning
- 1/4 cup olive oil
- 2 cloves garlic, minced
- 1 tablespoon Worcestershire sauce

Instructions:

1. **Marinate the Shrimp**
   In a bowl, combine shrimp, Cajun seasoning, olive oil, garlic, and Worcestershire sauce. Let marinate for 30 minutes.
2. **Cook the Shrimp**
   Preheat grill to medium-high heat. Skewer shrimp and grill for 2-3 minutes per side until pink.
3. **Serve**
   Serve hot with a squeeze of lemon.

BBQ Spatchcock Chicken

Ingredients:

- 1 whole chicken (3-4 lbs)
- 1/4 cup olive oil
- 2 tablespoons smoked paprika
- 1 tablespoon garlic powder
- Salt and pepper to taste
- 1 cup BBQ sauce

Instructions:

1. **Prepare the Chicken**
   Preheat grill to medium heat. Spatchcock the chicken by removing the backbone and flattening it.
2. **Season the Chicken**
   Rub the chicken with olive oil, paprika, garlic powder, salt, and pepper.
3. **Grill the Chicken**
   Place the chicken skin-side down on the grill. Cook for 45-60 minutes, flipping halfway and basting with BBQ sauce.
4. **Serve**
   Let rest before slicing and serving with additional BBQ sauce.

BBQ Pork Belly

Ingredients:

- 2 lbs pork belly, skin scored
- 1/4 cup BBQ rub (brown sugar, chili powder)
- 1 cup BBQ sauce

Instructions:

1. **Season the Pork Belly**
   Rub pork belly with BBQ rub and let it sit for at least 1 hour.
2. **Cook the Pork Belly**
   Preheat grill to low heat (about 225°F or 107°C). Place pork belly on the grill, skin-side up, and cook for 3-4 hours until tender.
3. **Finish with Sauce**
   Brush with BBQ sauce during the last 30 minutes of cooking. Let rest before slicing.
4. **Serve**
   Serve with additional BBQ sauce.

BBQ Beer Can Chicken

Ingredients:

- 1 whole chicken (3-4 lbs)
- 1 can beer (or soda)
- 1/4 cup BBQ rub (salt, paprika, garlic powder)
- 1 cup BBQ sauce

Instructions:

1. **Prepare the Chicken**
   Preheat grill to medium heat. Season chicken inside and out with BBQ rub.
2. **Insert the Beer Can**
   Open the beer can and place it inside the chicken's cavity.
3. **Grill the Chicken**
   Place the chicken upright on the grill and cook for 1-1.5 hours until the internal temperature reaches 165°F (74°C). Baste with BBQ sauce during the last 15 minutes.
4. **Serve**
   Carefully remove the beer can and let the chicken rest before serving.

BBQ Baked Potatoes

Ingredients:

- 4 large russet potatoes
- 1/4 cup olive oil
- Salt and pepper to taste
- 1 cup shredded cheese
- Sour cream and chives for serving

Instructions:

1. **Prepare the Potatoes**
   Preheat grill to medium heat. Rub potatoes with olive oil, salt, and pepper.
2. **Grill the Potatoes**
   Wrap potatoes in aluminum foil and place them on the grill. Cook for 45-60 minutes, turning occasionally, until tender.
3. **Finish and Serve**
   Unwrap and top with cheese, sour cream, and chives before serving.

BBQ Nachos

Ingredients:

- 1 bag tortilla chips
- 1 cup shredded cheese (cheddar, Monterey Jack)
- 1 cup pulled pork or chicken
- 1/2 cup BBQ sauce
- Toppings (jalapeños, sour cream, green onions)

Instructions:

1. **Assemble the Nachos**
   On a baking sheet, layer tortilla chips, cheese, pulled pork, and drizzle with BBQ sauce.
2. **Grill the Nachos**
   Preheat grill to medium heat. Place the baking sheet on the grill and cook for 5-7 minutes until cheese is melted.
3. **Add Toppings and Serve**
   Remove from the grill and top with jalapeños, sour cream, and green onions before serving.

BBQ Bacon-Wrapped Jalapeños

Ingredients:

- 12 jalapeños, halved and seeded
- 8 oz cream cheese, softened
- 1 cup shredded cheddar cheese
- 12 slices bacon, cut in half
- BBQ sauce for brushing

Instructions:

1. **Prepare Jalapeños**
   Preheat grill to medium heat. In a bowl, mix cream cheese and cheddar cheese. Fill each jalapeño half with the cheese mixture.
2. **Wrap with Bacon**
   Wrap each stuffed jalapeño with a half slice of bacon and secure with a toothpick.
3. **Grill**
   Place on the grill and cook for 15-20 minutes, brushing with BBQ sauce, until bacon is crispy.
4. **Serve**
   Serve hot as an appetizer.

BBQ Stuffed Peppers

Ingredients:

- 4 bell peppers (any color)
- 1 lb ground beef or turkey
- 1 cup cooked rice
- 1 cup BBQ sauce
- 1 cup shredded cheese

Instructions:

1. **Prepare the Peppers**
   Preheat grill to medium heat. Cut the tops off the bell peppers and remove seeds.
2. **Make the Filling**
   In a skillet, cook ground meat until browned. Mix in cooked rice and 1/2 cup BBQ sauce.
3. **Stuff the Peppers**
   Fill each bell pepper with the meat mixture and place them on the grill.
4. **Cook**
   Cover and grill for 30-35 minutes. Top with cheese during the last 5 minutes of cooking.
5. **Serve**
   Drizzle with remaining BBQ sauce before serving.

BBQ Sweet Potato Wedges

Ingredients:

- 4 large sweet potatoes, cut into wedges
- 2 tablespoons olive oil
- 1 tablespoon smoked paprika
- Salt and pepper to taste
- 1/4 cup BBQ sauce

Instructions:

1. **Preheat Grill**
   Preheat grill to medium heat.
2. **Season the Wedges**
   In a bowl, toss sweet potato wedges with olive oil, smoked paprika, salt, and pepper.
3. **Grill the Wedges**
   Place the wedges on the grill and cook for 20-25 minutes, turning occasionally, until tender.
4. **Add BBQ Sauce**
   Brush with BBQ sauce during the last few minutes of grilling.
5. **Serve**
   Serve hot as a side dish.

BBQ Burger Sliders

Ingredients:

- 1 lb ground beef
- 1/4 cup BBQ sauce
- Salt and pepper to taste
- 12 slider buns
- Toppings (cheese, pickles, onions)

Instructions:

1. **Make the Patties**
   In a bowl, mix ground beef, BBQ sauce, salt, and pepper. Form into 12 small patties.
2. **Grill the Patties**
   Preheat grill to medium heat. Grill patties for 3-4 minutes per side, adding cheese during the last minute if desired.
3. **Assemble the Sliders**
   Place patties on slider buns and add toppings of choice.
4. **Serve**
   Serve hot as appetizers or a main dish.

BBQ Fajitas

Ingredients:

- 1 lb flank steak, sliced
- 2 bell peppers, sliced
- 1 onion, sliced
- 1/4 cup olive oil
- 1/4 cup BBQ sauce
- Tortillas for serving

Instructions:

1. **Marinate the Steak**
   In a bowl, mix flank steak, bell peppers, onion, olive oil, and BBQ sauce. Let marinate for 30 minutes.
2. **Preheat Grill**
   Preheat grill to high heat.
3. **Grill the Fajitas**
   Grill the steak and vegetables for 5-7 minutes until cooked through.
4. **Serve**
   Serve with warm tortillas.

BBQ Meatball Subs

Ingredients:

- 1 lb ground beef
- 1/2 cup breadcrumbs
- 1/4 cup BBQ sauce
- 1 egg
- Salt and pepper to taste
- 6 sub rolls
- 1 cup shredded cheese

Instructions:

1. **Make the Meatballs**
   In a bowl, mix ground beef, breadcrumbs, BBQ sauce, egg, salt, and pepper. Form into meatballs.
2. **Preheat Grill**
   Preheat grill to medium heat. Grill meatballs for 10-12 minutes until cooked through.
3. **Assemble the Subs**
   Place meatballs in sub rolls and top with cheese.
4. **Melt the Cheese**
   Place subs on the grill for a few minutes to melt the cheese.
5. **Serve**
   Serve hot with additional BBQ sauce.

BBQ Mac and Cheese

Ingredients:

- 1 lb elbow macaroni
- 4 cups shredded cheese (cheddar, mozzarella)
- 2 cups milk
- 1/2 cup BBQ sauce
- 1/4 cup butter
- Salt and pepper to taste

Instructions:

1. **Cook the Pasta**
   Cook macaroni according to package instructions. Drain and set aside.
2. **Make the Cheese Sauce**
   In a saucepan, melt butter, add milk, and stir in cheese until melted. Mix in BBQ sauce and season with salt and pepper.
3. **Combine**
   Mix the cheese sauce with the cooked macaroni.
4. **Grill**
   Transfer to a grill-safe dish and place on the grill for 10-15 minutes, stirring occasionally.
5. **Serve**
   Serve hot as a side dish.

BBQ Pulled Pork Sandwiches

Ingredients:

- 3 lbs pork shoulder
- 1 cup BBQ rub
- 2 cups BBQ sauce
- 8 hamburger buns
- Coleslaw for topping

Instructions:

1. **Season the Pork**
   Rub pork shoulder with BBQ rub and let marinate for at least 1 hour.
2. **Cook the Pork**
   Preheat grill to low heat (about 225°F or 107°C). Place pork shoulder on the grill and cook for 6-8 hours until tender, basting with BBQ sauce.
3. **Shred the Pork**
   Remove from grill and let rest before shredding.
4. **Assemble the Sandwiches**
   Place pulled pork on hamburger buns and top with coleslaw.
5. **Serve**
   Serve hot with extra BBQ sauce on the side.

BBQ Deviled Eggs

Ingredients:

- 12 large eggs
- 1/2 cup mayonnaise
- 2 tablespoons BBQ sauce
- 1 teaspoon mustard
- Salt and pepper to taste
- Smoked paprika for garnish

Instructions:

1. **Boil the Eggs**
   Place eggs in a pot and cover with water. Bring to a boil, then remove from heat and let sit for 12 minutes.
2. **Cool and Peel**
   Transfer eggs to an ice bath to cool. Once cool, peel and slice in half lengthwise.
3. **Prepare Filling**
   Remove yolks and place in a bowl. Mash yolks with mayonnaise, BBQ sauce, mustard, salt, and pepper until smooth.
4. **Fill the Eggs**
   Spoon or pipe the filling back into the egg whites.
5. **Garnish and Serve**
   Sprinkle with smoked paprika and serve chilled as an appetizer.

BBQ Dessert Pizza

Ingredients:

- 1 pre-made pizza crust
- 1/2 cup BBQ sauce
- 1 cup shredded mozzarella cheese
- 1 cup sliced fresh fruits (such as strawberries, bananas, and peaches)
- 1/2 cup mini marshmallows
- 1/4 cup chopped nuts (optional)
- Honey for drizzling

Instructions:

1. **Preheat the Grill**
   Preheat grill to medium heat.
2. **Assemble the Pizza**
   Spread BBQ sauce over the pizza crust, then sprinkle with mozzarella cheese. Arrange sliced fruits and mini marshmallows on top.
3. **Grill the Pizza**
   Place the pizza on the grill and close the lid. Grill for 10-12 minutes until the cheese is melted and bubbly.
4. **Add Toppings**
   Remove from the grill and sprinkle with chopped nuts, if using. Drizzle with honey.
5. **Serve**
   Slice and serve warm as a fun dessert.

www.ingramcontent.com/pod-product-compliance
Lightning Source LLC
LaVergne TN
LVHW081330060526
838201LV00055B/2560